Other books by Daniel J. Simundson:

Where Is God in My Suffering?
The Message of Job
Faith under Fire

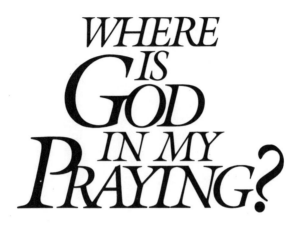

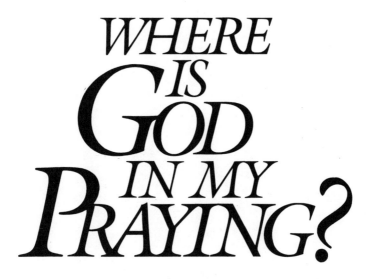

WHERE IS GOD IN MY PRAYING?

Biblical Responses to Eight Searching Questions

DANIEL J. SIMUNDSON

AUGSBURG Publishing House • Minneapolis

WHERE IS GOD IN MY PRAYING?
Biblical Responses to Eight Searching Questions

Copyright © 1986 Augsburg Publishing House

Scripture quotations unless otherwise noted are from the Holy Bible: New International Version. Copyright 1978 by the New York International Bible Society. Used by permission of Zondervan Bible Publishers.

Photos: Wallowitch, 24; Religious News Service, 34; APH Photo, 44; Rohn Engh, 64; Robert Maust, 74.

Library of Congress Cataloging-in-Publication Data

Simundson, Daniel J.
  WHERE IS GOD IN MY PRAYING?

  1. Prayer—Biblical teaching. I. Title.
BS680.P64S56   1986   248.3'2   86-22294
ISBN 0-8066-2241-5

Manufactured in the U.S.A.   APH 10-7096

1   2   3   4   5   6   7   8   9   0   1   2   3   4   5   6   7   8   9

To Susan and Ann Marie

Contents

Preface

Prayer is at the center of our faith. It is the place where we communicate with our God. On the one hand, it is the most simple of religious acts. On the other hand, it can be a complicated process that raises many questions for us: Where do I find God? How do I know God is listening? Do our prayers actually affect what God will do? Will God be angry with me for saying that? Does God really answer every prayer? If so, why didn't I receive what I asked for? Is it my fault—or God's?

In this book we will take a closer look at questions that are often raised regarding prayer. We will examine each question in the light of biblical passages, highlighting specific texts from the Old and New Testaments for each chapter.

This book could be used in a variety of ways. A pastor who is planning a series of sermons on prayer might find stimulation here. A class of teenagers or adults could make use of the book as they share with each other their own questions about prayer. Laypeople and pastors who think about their own prayer life and wish to grow in their understanding may find ideas here that will enliven their thinking.

Of course, it is more important to pray than it is to read or talk about prayer, but our understanding of prayer may hinder our prayer life, and new ideas may help to free us for a richer relationship with God. It is the author's hope that this book will serve in some modest way toward that end.

CHAPTER ONE

GENESIS 1:26-27
MATTHEW 6:9-13

Why Should I Pray?

Sharon and David both go to the same church. They have known each other since childhood. They both learned their Sunday school lessons from Mrs. Johnson and were taught by Pastor Robertson. They are both active, faithful church members, serving on several boards and committees and teaching Sunday school. But in spite of all these similarities, they are very different in their approach to prayer.

Sharon is disciplined about her prayer life. Every morning and every night she sets aside time for Bible study, reading her devotional booklet, and speaking directly to God. She would probably never ask the question, "Why should I pray?" She prays just because it is the thing to do. She can't imagine not praying.

David prays before supper (or, to be more precise, one of the children does) and in Sunday morning service (actually, the pastor does), but most of the time he doesn't even think about prayer. In an occasional tight spot, he finds himself muttering a request for help from God—but that seems almost like a reflex action, something left over from his childhood, rather than a formal prayer. David considers himself a good Christian. He believes in God and works in the church, but he seldom engages in what we would call prayer: talking with God, meditating, listening quietly for a response from God. Most of the time, this omission doesn't bother him. But, on occasion, especially when confronted by the example of someone like Sharon, he wonders if something is lacking in his religious life. Is he missing something? If so, what? Why should he pray?

For some, prayer is easy and natural, and they seldom ask such a question. For others, prayer is minimal, and, if they occasionally attempt it, the prayer seems difficult and forced. They ask, "Why should I pray? Is it to my advantage? or God's? or both?"

1.   *God created us to be in communication with him.*

God made us human beings with the possibility of communicating with our Creator. God must have wanted it that way. Surely God could have made a world in which all creatures merely act as God demands, as a puppeteer twitches his hand to make the puppet jump to the bidding of the one who controls everything. Or, God could have set the world in motion, wound up the automatic timing device, checked to see that all the cause-and-effect relationships were in good working order, and then departed to some remote corner of the universe to be preoccupied with other interests. But God did not do it that way. God wants involvement with the creatures that God made—perhaps even with the plants and animals, but most surely with the human beings. We are created in God's image. And whatever else that means, it seems that we are born to communicate with God— to be responsible, to share our thoughts and feelings, to seek fulfillment by connecting with the one who made us.

God wants us to have a relationship with him, and no relationship can flourish without communication. How can two persons grow in understanding and affection toward one another if they never speak? On the human level, we are reminded again and again of the importance of communication—whether we are talking about how families work, or politicians govern, or business executives run a company, or coaches develop a winning team. Similarly, if our communication with God is limited to occasional cries for help when we sense danger, or a perfunctory word of thanks before our evening meal, or a list of "gimmes" addressed to a celestial Santa Claus, then we do not have a very close relationship with God.

Some people who consider themselves religious do not spend much time in *structured* prayer, but they say that, in a sense, they are praying all the time. If they work at the Christian life, seeking ways to serve God and others, they may say that their whole life is a prayer. God is close to them and with them, even if they do not consciously stop and take the time to speak to God in a "traditional" prayer. There is, of course, truth to this.

Others say that our prayers need not be verbal— words and sentences that directly address God. We can communicate through all the senses. Perhaps God is closest to us as we watch a sunset at the lake, or listen to a Bach cantata, or touch the hand of a loved one, or admire a sleeping baby, or relax in a big chair by the fire with a purring cat in our lap.

Some ask, must prayer always be articulated in clearly definable language? What about a little mystery and awe and feeling?

Surely, all of life can be a prayer. Certainly, we communicate with God, as with other people, in many nonverbal ways. And yet, as with a husband and wife who never talk to each other about things that really matter, there is something lacking in the life of a human being who never takes time to speak with God. God made us to communicate with him. That communication ought to be natural and spontaneous, especially for those who openly profess belief in God. But for many of us it is not.

2.   *As vulnerable human beings, we need God.*

It can be tough to be a human being. Like God's other creatures, we are mortal. We are here for a while, and then we are gone. For ages and ages we did not exist, and after our brief time in the sun, the world will get along very well without us, as it did before we came. But unlike other creatures (at least as far as we can tell), we human beings know about our mortality. And so even our brief experience of life is marred by our fear of death, our terror of nonexistence, our wondering whether there is anything beyond this, and our hope that we will not be held accountable in some future life for all our shortcomings in this one. Life is short, to be sure—and not always pleasant. There are many dangers that can hurt us as we move toward its inevitable end.

In a transient world such as this, we are in need of some stability, something that does not change, one who is good and reliable. We need assurance of a good God who is involved in our present and to whom we can hand over our future. Since so much is out of our own control, we want to believe in a God who has some final say about how everything will turn out. We need a God to whom we can speak honestly about our weakness, one to whom we can admit our fear and vulnerability, confident that he will not use our weakness against us but rather will protect and keep us.

Prayer often takes the form of crying out to God in times of great trouble, asking for help and hope. Since we human beings walk a perilous journey between birth and death, it is not unusual that a cry for help is often the context and content of our prayers. In fact, many think of praying only in times of trouble. The rest of the time, when they are making it on their own, they perceive no need for God.

It is clearly appropriate to call out to God for help. The problem is that it is hard to talk to God if we are not accustomed to it. What kind of relationship do I have with my friends if I call only when I am in trouble and want something from them?

3.   *God has told us to pray.*

We should pray because God has told us to pray. It is a command, not simply a word of advice to be accepted or rejected. God knows we need to pray. God wants to carry on a meaningful relationship with us. The Bible abounds with admonitions, invitations, and exhortations to pray. As believers who want to be faithful, who desire to do what is right, who are called to be obedient servants, we cannot dismiss this word from God lightly—anymore than we can ignore other imperatives from God.

So we need a little discipline. We can trust that what God expects from us is for our own good and is not an arbitrary rule that God imposes simply to prove his authority over us. Maybe we should force ourselves to pray, to do it because it is required, to carry on a prayer life even when we don't feel like it or have nothing to say or don't really know if God is listening. A good prayer life may require work, discipline, and pushing ahead even if it isn't going so well, even when we seem to be only going through the motions.

God does not simply drop a demand on us and then leave us to struggle with our inability to pray. God teaches us to pray. If we cannot find the words that are appropriate, God will provide them. Jesus taught his disciples how to pray. In the words of the Lord's Prayer, he gave us both form and content as a model for our own praying. We are to be concerned for God's name and the coming of God's kingdom. By praying that God's will may be done we are both asking for God to work for that goal and accepting the responsibility to do our own part to accomplish God's will. We are also invited to pray for our own needs, both physical and spiritual, bread and forgiveness. And we may also ask for help in avoiding the hazards of this life, whether brought on by our own succumbing to temptation or by evil outside us that wishes to hurt us.

The great variety of psalms in the Bible is also a gift from God and our religious predecessors. No matter what our present circumstance, there is a word there that can help us in our praying. Whether ours is a time of joy or sorrow, God wants to hear from us, to share in our experience, to rejoice with us and to weep with us. Even when prayer is most difficult, when God seems absent and we are in great spiritual turmoil, God helps us to find the words—even if they be only words of doubt or anger—"How long, O Lord?" or "Why have you forsaken me?"

God commands us to pray—to keep talking and not turn our backs. God has given us models of prayer and words to use so that we need not retreat in silence even when we are tongue-tied with despair or frightened into muteness by our anger.

God has promised to listen and come to our aid. Just as God heard the cry of the Hebrew slaves in

Egypt, the frustrations of Moses, the repentance of David, the loneliness of Jeremiah, the humiliation of the exiles, or the desperation of those who scrambled after Jesus seeking healing, so God will hear us. God would not command us to pray if God were not prepared to listen. "Talk to me," God says. "Tell me what is going on with you. Speak up. Don't be afraid. Say what you really think and feel. Get it out in the open so we can look at it and understand it and do something about it."

4.   *We follow the example of other persons of faith.*

We pray because that is what persons of faith have always done. We have been left with a powerful example by those who have preceded us in the family of faith—in the pages of the Old and New Testaments, in the martyrs and reformers throughout the history of the church, and in the lives of those whom we have known personally (the pious grandmother, the favorite pastor, the youth leader, the chronic sufferer).

All the great biblical characters were people of prayer. They talked to God, and God talked to them. Adam and Eve talked with God in the garden. Abraham heard God's voice and obediently moved into the unknown. Jacob's communication with God at times was a great struggle, as if he and God were contenders in a wrestling match. Joseph, Moses, Miriam, Deborah, David, Jeremiah, Daniel—the list could go on and on.

Jesus was constantly in conversation with God. Sometimes Jesus needed to be away for a while, far from the crowds with their demands on his time and strength, in order to concentrate on his relationship with his Father. But at all times, in the midst of daily life, when confronted by the pain and suffering of other human beings, when sharing their joy, and when facing his own death in Gethsemane and on that horrible cross, a prayer was in his mind and on his tongue. Jesus not only taught us to pray by providing form and content, but also by his example of a human being who lives a life of prayer.

Why should we pray? For some, prayer is so natural that the question seems unnecessary. But for many of us, who have a sneaking suspicion that our prayer life is not quite what it could be, it is a question worth contemplating. Thanks be to God who has made us with the need and ability to communicate with our Maker and who will not let us alone until we turn to him.

CHAPTER TWO

GENESIS 3:8-10
ROMANS 8:26-27

Why Is It
So Hard to Pray?

Prayer should be natural and spontaneous for a human being. After all, God made us to have communication with him. We need that relationship with the one who is everlasting and good because we live in a world that is transient and sometimes evil. God has told us to pray—for our own good.

Yet many of us find it difficult to pray. We know our prayer life is not what it could be. Examples of other believers who do better at praying than we do only make us feel guilty.

Perhaps it will help if we think about some of the reasons why prayer has become a difficult chore for many. Why is it so hard to pray?

1. *Our relationship with God has been broken by sin.*

Something has gone wrong in the relationship between God and human beings. Pride, distrust, and
disobedience turned the idyllic scene in the garden
into a tragedy. The man and the woman did not take
God at his word. God had given them a wide range
of freedom but had told them that there was one thing
they should not do: "Stay away from that tree in the
middle of the garden or you will die." The seed of
distrust was already in their minds: "Why is God denying us the freedom to eat from this tree? Is God
trying to keep us ignorant and subservient? Is God
afraid that we might find out something for ourselves
that will make us less dependent on him?" Pride fueled
the distrust. Pride drives us into discontent about our
humanity, our limitations of understanding, and our
control of our destiny. We want to know it ourselves
and do it ourselves. "Maybe God doesn't really have
our best interests in mind after all," we think. "What
is the real reason God forbids certain things? How can
we trust God?" Pride and distrust then lead to disobedience, and disobedience leads to guilt.

In such a relationship, now disturbed by distrust
and guilt, conversation will be strained and difficult.
In fact, we will try to avoid encounter altogether, so
that we do not reveal what is really bothering us. And
so, like the first man and woman, we hide from the
presence of the Lord among the trees of the garden.
We know that we are naked, and we fear that God will
see us as we really are. If God chases us down and

demands that we speak, we prefer to talk about what is insubstantial—the weather, or the pennant potential of the local baseball team, an inconsequential sin of indiscretion, or some abstract theological doctrine—in order to keep the conversation away from matters that are really important to us. As in our human communication, we find it difficult to speak freely and openly and to bare our soul with those whom we do not completely trust.

2.   In our modern, secular world, it is hard to see the presence and working of God.

How do you picture God when you shut your eyes to pray? Does God look like a human being—someone familiar, approachable, friendly? Perhaps he looks to you like an old, graying Jesus, or maybe you imagine a loving old grandmother. But is any human image of God adequate? Is not God above and beyond anything that we can see?

Where is God to be found these days? Does God live in heaven? But where is that? The astronauts have been up there now, and they have not seen God anywhere. The universe has become so complex for us that the old images of God and heaven and earth seem rather crude and unsophisticated. It is hard to picture God or locate God.

Scientists present us with elaborate cause-and-effect theories to explain what is going on in the universe, and one wonders how God fits into all this. The big bang theory of the formation of the universe, the long evolution of living species, the meteorological reason for a drought, the sociological causes of war, the psychological determinants in various mental disorders—these are all ways of explaining what is going on in the world without any reference to God. It seems that God is not necessary any more. The idea of a God who takes direct action in all that happens, who intervenes on our behalf, who heals diseases and transforms evil persons and feeds the hungry is hard to maintain. We modern people look for explanations that we can see and document and test. And so there is little room for the supernatural. How can you test to see if God or the doctor or the medicine or one's positive outlook was the major factor in one's return to health?

Many tend to think of God language as the fall-back position, the explanation that we use only if we do not have a better one. The more we learn, the less we need God. There is considerable pressure from others to abandon our "primitive" (or even "superstitious") beliefs in God and to come along into the 20th century. Belief in the supernatural—the mysterious—has become difficult for many people. Obviously, if you do not believe in God, if God has been almost totally removed from daily life, then it is hard to pray to God.

We modern people have done a good job figuring out how the world works. We can explain all sorts of things that would have mystified our grandparents, let alone our biblical ancestors. But sometimes we treat our partial answers as if they had plumbed the depths of the mystery of existence. Psychological theories that help us predict human behavior, true and helpful though they be, do not adequately explain sin, forgiveness, reconciliation, and the possibility of a new life.

Medicines and surgical practices developed by the hard work of dedicated scientists may *also* be the work of God. Though we give the credit to human beings, we need not eliminate God's participation. It is true that God's action cannot be proved. And in the mind-set of our day, that tends to make God (if God exists at all) remotely distant. Prayer, then, becomes difficult, if not hopelessly out of date.

3.   *We worry about what we should say.*

With persons we don't really know very well, or don't quite trust, we tend to be careful about what we say. The conversation lacks spontaneity and naturalness. We become more preoccupied with our own words than with the other person. We critique our words even as we say them, and our communication becomes awkward. We are more concerned with how we are heard than with an honest presentation of our own thoughts and feelings.

Prayer is difficult for many because they are too concerned about what they should say. What is legitimate content for our prayers? Are there some things that are proper issues to bring before the Almighty, but others that are not worthy of God's concern? Are there some things better left unsaid because they might reveal too much about ourselves? We wonder if God will take offense, give us a bad grade on our theological understanding, or be critical of our selfishness or pettiness.

Public prayer is a particularly difficult for many of us. Though we may have developed a private style of prayer that is fairly free and open toward God, we don't want any other human beings listening in on our prayer. In some churches, a pastor would seldom call on a person for the prayer to open a meeting without a word of warning ahead of time. And some people make it clear that they never want to be asked. If invited to pray in a group, some feel much safer when using written prayers or those committed to memory during childhood. Again, we are concerned more with how our words are received than we are with praying what is on our mind and heart.

We have a particularly hard time finding the right words when our true thoughts and feelings do not match what we think *should* be the correct attitude of one who comes to God in prayer. We find it very difficult, for example, to express negative emotions to anyone, particularly to God. We have learned that one should come to God in a repentant mood, willing to confess sins, praising and giving thanks to God, and then, after all these preliminaries are taken care of, it is all right to ask for a few things that we need (maybe even a few trivial wants, if we don't pile the list up too high). But we don't know how to pray if we are not in a thankful or praising mood, if we are angry at God rather than grateful to God, if we do not feel particularly repentant, or if we have a selfish request to lay before God. How can we talk to God if we believe that what we have to say is an unacceptable prayer? How can we be honest with God if we dare not tell God what is really our chief concern? And if prayer is not honest communication, then there really is little point in it.

Prayer is hard for us because we worry too much about saying it right instead of simply saying it.

4. We have had our prayer requests denied or ignored in the past.

Many people have stopped praying, or at least have found it more difficult, because of some vivid experience in which they have asked God for something with great fervor, inspired by biblical texts that promise God will answer, only to have that request denied—or at least it seemed that way. It may have been a rather minor issue early in life—the Christmas bike that never materialized, the kitten that died anyway, the lost football that was never recovered—but in some way it was the end of naivete. Life was never so simple again. We learned that you can pray with the kind of faith that moves mountains and you still might not get what you ask for.

For others, the experience may be much deeper and more tragic. The young father prays that the doctor's dreadful prognosis will be a mistake, that some miracle will occur to overturn the terrible odds, that God will hear and act—but his child dies anyway. And it is never the same again between that father and God.

How is the one who has been terribly disappointed by a no from God supposed to think about prayer? What about those promises to "Ask and you shall receive?" For many such persons, prayer has lost its value. They may become terribly skeptical (if not cynical) about the efficacy of prayer. If, as many think, prayer is primarily a process of presenting your petitions before God in the hopes that you will receive what you have requested, then a no from God makes prayer difficult. Once one has been burned, the scar never quite goes away.

For some, the experience of a "failed" prayer is slightly different. They have prayed with great passion and persistence, assaulting heaven with their concerns, but have been met only with silence. It was as if God were absent, not even listening. Even a clear no seems preferable to them than a cold silence in which all they can hear are their own words drifting off into space. It is bad enough if God will not grant our requests. Perhaps we can come up with a rationalization that helps us make sense out of that. But if God will not even listen, if God will not hear us out, if God seems to turn away or go off to some other galaxy, leaving us to writhe alone in our pain, then we wonder if there is any reason whatsoever to take it to the Lord in prayer.

For many reasons, it is hard for us to pray. Our broken relationships with others and with God have made all honest communication difficult. Our modern, scientific age seems to compound the problems of being in touch with the divine. We worry about what to say rather than being natural and open. And, to a greater or lesser degree, we have had experiences of "unanswered" prayer.

5.   *When prayer is the most difficult for us, the Spirit prays for us.*

We will need to return later to a fuller discussion of some of these issues that make it hard for us to pray.

At this time it is sufficient to say that God does not leave us in our state of isolation, burdened with our inability to communicate with God. In the words of Paul, though we are weak and do not know how to pray as we ought, "the Spirit himself intercedes for us with groans that words cannot express" (Rom. 8:26). Even when we cannot form the words, the prayer goes on. And God, who searches human hearts and knows what is the mind of the Spirit, will graciously hear the prayer that we could not even utter on our own.

CHAPTER THREE

JOB 1:20
MATTHEW 6:5-8

Must We All
Pray the Same Way?

One of the most significant issues that separates Christians is their approach to prayer. Churches may divide and redivide over lofty theological disputes about justification, the person of Jesus, or the authority of Scripture, but the place where differences become apparent to most believers is in the way people pray. And we are not reluctant to express our opinions about how others are doing it: "*Those* people don't know how to pray unless they read a prayer written by somebody else, preferably someone who died at least 300 years ago." Or, "*Those* people don't know how to pray without waving their hands in the air and looking like they've worked themselves into a hypnotic trance."

One person thinks it attracts too much attention to

join hands and pray at a restaurant ("Didn't Jesus tell us to pray in a closet by ourselves?") while another person thinks that such a public display of piety is a good witness to others that we are practicing Christians.

When Job tore his robe and shaved his head and fell on the ground to lament the loss of his property and children, he was not doing anything unusual for persons of his time who expressed such grief. But in our day and culture such behavior would be considered bizarre, no matter how severe the provocation, and we would wonder if poor Job had lost his mind.

Many are convinced that their way of praying is the only way and that all who deviate from their understanding of the norm are surely deficient in their relationship with God. It is not uncommon for someone to leave what they describe as a "cold, formal, unfeeling" church to discover a community where people are warm and the Spirit is at work. They may not leave their relatives and friends alone until they, too, see the light, break out of their cocoon, and join them.

But must we all pray the same way? Is there no room for diversity? May not people express the uniqueness of their personalities in the way they relate to God? Are there not different occasions in life that call for a variety of prayers—both with regard to style and content?

Let us look at the legitimacy of diversity in prayer from several different perspectives.

1.   Prayer changes as situations change.

Everything I say is affected by the way I feel, what is happening to me, and how hopeful I am. When I am happy, my friends know it because it comes through to them. I am much easier to live with some days than others.

It is easy to praise God when life is good and everything is going my way. Life has its wonderful experiences of joy, belonging, love, security, and trust. At times I want to sing about what a wonderful world this is—when the weather is perfect, my job is rewarding, there are people whom I love and who also love me, and my faith in God is strong.

But life also has its low points. Unfortunately, some people have more of these than others—but few lives avoid at least an occasional walk through some dark valley. When we talk to others (whether to God or to human beings) in times of despair and grief and fear, our conversations will surely be different than they are on the sunny, optimistic days. It is hard to praise God in the midst of disaster.

One kind of prayer cannot suffice for the variety of human experiences. One would not say the same prayer at both a wedding and a funeral. Our prayer should reflect what we feel and think at a particular moment. Because our circumstances change, so must our prayer.

So, if we have been taught that we should always pray with a sombre face and downturned eyes and extended confessions of our sins, we may stifle the joy that is in our hearts as we feel compelled to pray a prayer that does not fit us.

On the other hand, it is cruel to insist that a person in great torment, grieving the loss of a loved one or the bad news of a terminal illness or a deteriorating marriage, must offer praise and thanks to God *anyway*.

That would be like telling Job to get up off the ground and put his clothes back on and quit acting in such a negative manner: "Come on, Job. Don't you believe in God? Give praise and thanks to God for what you still have. This experience will be good for you." It is true that Job needed to pray, to keep the conversation with God alive, but Job needed to pray what *he* felt and thought, not what someone else told him was an appropriate prayer for a religious person at such a time.

Several components often show up in our prayers— petition, intercession, confession, thanksgiving, and adoration. But each prayer need not contain all of them. Over a period of time, a balanced prayer life will probably touch on all of these areas, but in a given situation, one might be locked into a particular kind of prayer and find it difficult to think about anything else. A woman whose husband is going through a critical postsurgical recuperation will focus on prayers of intercession. She is almost completely preoccupied with pleas for a full recovery of the one she loves, frightened by the loneliness and grief that would accompany his death. Because she cannot bear to think of this, her prayer is one-sided. Only later will she be able to think of other issues to raise with God.

The book of Psalms contains a rich variety of prayers, both for individuals and for use by the whole community, that help us find words appropriate for any situation in which we find ourselves. There are hymns of praise, psalms of thanksgiving, laments, and more. We know that prayers of praise and thanksgiving are expected of Christians, but we are not so sure that laments are fitting for those who claim to trust in God. They seem too negative and doubting for use by a "true" believer. And so we often turn away from the biblical resources that are available to us. We will need to return for a closer look at the laments.

Our prayers are not always the same, because our life situations change. What was an appropriate prayer for us at one point in our life may not be at another.

2.   Both spontaneous and written prayers are important.

Some people are convinced that prayer should be spontaneous, open to the Spirit, and unencumbered by formal ritual or archaic language. They believe that one should be able to speak to God directly, without relying on the crutch of other people's prayers. They admire ministers who can pray their own prayers rather than reading the same old words out of a book week after week. According to this view, familiarity and constant repetition lead to distraction, boredom, and superficiality. Prayer then becomes a rote recitation of empty words, spoken without even thinking. Even the Lord's Prayer can be said while a person thinks about something else.

Others believe that we should not shrug off the great liturgies and prayers of those believers who have gone before us. In their view, a prayer that has been shaped and fine-tuned over centuries of use can probably say it better than the words that we speak glibly off the top of our heads.

Then, too, many who think they are saying fresh, new prayers every week may actually be repeating themselves almost as much as if they were reading the prayer from an order of service. A friend who is a member of a church that prides itself on pastors who can pray for 15 minutes at a time without benefit of written notes says that he heard essentially the same "free" prayer three times in one year, in three different parts of the country.

Perhaps both sides are right. We ought to be able to pray our own prayer, to be spontaneous and natural in our approach to God, and not to hide behind some-one else's words. But it is also true that we can gain from what others have prayed, whether in Bible times, in our own time, or in the many years in between. We are not the first people who have believed in Christ and have tried to keep in touch with God. What we think is "free" prayer may actually be redundant and not very well thought-out. We need a mix of both kinds of prayer—certainly in our private devotions and prob-ably also in our public worship.

3. *Is discipline necessary?*

At the end of their first year of study, we often ask seminarians, "What can you tell us about your own discipline of prayer?" Most of the time it is a rather embarrassing question. Most respond with apologies that they are still working at their prayer life and hope it gets better. Some students are rebelling against what has seemed to them to be a rigid, legalistic, conforming, or mechanistic piety. Others have no example either to follow or reject, having grown up in families where no one prayed except in church and sometimes at meals. Some are rebelling against the discipline they have known, while others are groping for some method to order their prayer life.

We tend to react against religious demands. To many Christians, law, obligation, and discipline seem like bad words. Though God has told us to pray, we resist setting up a schedule. We pray when the occasion arises, when the Spirit moves us. We don't want to turn our prayer life into a duty, a job to be done. We don't want to think of it as "putting in our time."

But a discipline of prayer may be important for us. We should not limit our praying to those times when we feel the urge, when we are in the mood and not distracted by our busy lives. If we do, we may never pray.

Discipline means praying regularly at specific times and places, perhaps following a similar routine, possibly adopting certain postures like kneeling, standing, or using breathing exercises. Though it may seem legalistic and superficial, such consistency in prayer may be quite helpful.

As we have already noted, there are many reasons why prayer can become difficult. It is especially important to have an ordered prayer life at those times when the hindrances to prayer are particularly strong. A disciplined life of prayer can keep the connections with God open even when God's presence is not so clear and our need to pray is not so obvious.

4.   We need to pray alone and in groups.

It is always appropriate to talk directly to God, by ourselves, just God and us, without the help of any intermediaries and with no one listening over our shoulder. Jesus even said that we should get off by ourselves into a closet instead of making a show by praying out in public to enhance our own reputation. The hypocrites did that—and those who believe they can pray on their own without the benefit of the church are quick to tell us that the church is full of hypocrites.

But surely Jesus did not mean that we should never gather together to pray with other believers, that our praying should always be private. Through prayer we are bound to others. We learned how to pray from other human beings. Our first prayers were learned by heart from people who loved us and whose word we trusted. We pray with others at table, at a child's bedside, at the grave, and in the worship service. Our praying reminds us of our mutual dependence on each other and God. Communal prayer brings to remembrance those in great need. Persons who are in trouble are greatly comforted to know that others are praying for them.

In recognition of our need for a variety of prayers, the book of Psalms contains prayers that are meant to be offered by the whole community, as well as those that center on the needs of individuals. We have many experiences in common, and there is strength in coming together to share with God and each other, rather than for each individual to bring his or her prayer in a separate and private conversation.

A life of prayer is both an individual matter and a communal process.

5.   *The Bible recognizes our diversity.*

We need not all pray the same way. The important thing is to pray, to talk to God, and to be honest in our communication. We differ from each other in many ways. Your prayer may be wrong for me, and the prayer that flows from my personality would be out of place on your lips.

Furthermore, I will not pray the same prayer in all circumstances. When I am happy, my talk will show that. When I am grieving, I cannot pretend to be happy. At times my prayer will be spontaneous, open, and trusting. I can talk to God easily and I know I am heard. At times, the only thing that keeps me praying at all is my discipline in sticking to it even when nothing seems to be happening.

Sometimes God and I need to be alone. At other times I need the comfort and support of fellow believers.

All of this variety is represented in the Bible. We have referred to the many kinds of prayer, both communal and individual, in the book of Psalms. Job, Jesus, and countless other biblical personalities show us that there is not a "right" or "wrong" prayer. What is important is a relationship with God that allows us to be true to ourselves and our present circumstances and to be free to share that with God.

CHAPTER FOUR

JOB 7:11-21
MARK 15:33-34

Can I Tell God
What I Really Think?

Sometimes we wonder about ourselves when we compare the serenity and unwavering faith of other Christians with the anger, frustration, disappointment, and doubts that we see in our own relationship with God. How should we deal with such thoughts and feelings? We are embarrassed by them or feel guilty about them.

Why can't we be like those positive, smiling, upbeat people on religious TV programs? Why can't we be like those writers of autobiographies on sale at Christian bookstores? People who have endured much more suffering than we have still manage to stay strong and trusting and have kept their emotions under control.

Our friends tell us that if we think positively, things will get better. They support us when we grit our teeth and mask our pain, but they tell us we shouldn't think like that when we let slip even a hint of the doubts and fears that lurk under the surface. And so we cannot admit our struggles even to our friends.

How then can we be honest with God? Will God not punish us for our lack of faith, our preoccupation with self, our hostility toward God and others?

So we keep quiet. We hide our negative thoughts and emotions from family and friends, and we try to do the same with God. We may have some success in putting on a good front with our friends, but those who know us best can probably see through our pretense, read our body language, sense our irritability, and know that we are not really as upbeat as we pretend. If we cannot fool our human acquaintances, are we able to fool God? We often act as if God almighty does not already know what we are thinking and how we are feeling, as if refusing to talk about it is the way to keep it secret from the one who reads even our inmost heart.

Let us look at two examples of biblical prayers that some persons might find objectionable. One was prayed by Job; the other, by Jesus.

1.   Should Job have prayed like this?

Job was the model of a good, religious, successful, respected person. Then disasters came, one after the other, until he was left alone, without property or children or health or human consolation, squatting unceremoniously on an ash heap at the edge of town, scratching his open sores with a piece of a broken pot.

At first he reacted as we might expect such a good, pious man to act. He made some brave statements about praising the Lord and being able to take whatever the Lord brings, whether good or evil. He seemed to remain strong in his faith, a good example to other believers who might some day have to endure such an ordeal.

But then he began to wonder: why had God done this to him? His friends tried to tell him that there was probably some good reason—either that he deserved it because of some sin that he had been reluctant to confess, or that he might learn something that would make him a better human being.

But Job refused to accept such condemning interpretations of his condition. He turned to God, not to confess his sins, as his friends suggested, but to complain. And so his prayer in Job 7:11-21 is a lament, a prayer uttered by one in great trouble, an attempt to be honest with God about his dilemma.

Those who desire to keep our conversation with God on a high level and avoid any hint of negativism would have several criticisms of Job's prayer.

Job's attitude was "wrong." In v. 11, Job said he could not restrain himself; he must complain. That, in itself, would be unacceptable to some pious critics. Who are we mere mortals to complain to God? We have no right. We don't know enough. Only God sees the large picture, so stop complaining and start believing.

In vv. 15-16, Job talked about how he would rather be dead than to continue his present existence. He hated his life.

Confronted by such a morbid, complaining attitude, most of us, like Job's counselors, feel compelled to try to change the mind of a person like Job. We might try to talk him out of it, point out something positive about his situation, or attempt to cheer him up. We would not want to let the complaint continue. We would not want to listen to it. We would not think it was doing the sufferer any good. We would wish the person were "taking it" better, and would be disappointed that he wasn't.

Job accused God of many nasty things. Job said that God was paying too much attention to him, treating him as if he were a threat (like a great sea monster, v. 12) rather than just a puny mortal. Job went to bed at night, hoping to find in sleep at least temporary relief from his pain, but God came to scare him with nightmares (vv. 13-14). God wouldn't let Job alone for a minute (vv. 16, 19), and Job wondered why God had singled him out for such cruel treatment. Even if Job were a sinner, why is that such a big deal to God (v. 20)?

Should one talk to God like this? Was Job right? Does God take delight in tormenting defenseless human beings?

Of course, we do not believe that God is cruel and was deliberately torturing Job. But that is not really the point. Whether Job was right or wrong is not the main issue. What is important is that Job thought that God was "out to get him." It seemed that way as he reflected on the meaninglessness of his terrible situation, his confidence that he was innocent and that God was all-powerful. So he told God what he thought, and that is what a prayer should be. That is why Job's prayer is a legitimate one, a conversation that was able to bring out into the open what was happening in the relationship between God and Job.

One would not choose to copy Job. We would hope that we could be spared such thoughts about God. But if the thoughts are already there, Job's prayer is a reminder that it is better to say it to God than to pretend that all is well when it isn't.

2. How could Jesus say such things?

It's one thing to criticize the way Job prayed (or, similarly, Moses or David or Jeremiah). After all, they were Old Testament characters. And they were clearly human beings, revealing their creaturely flaws in other ways besides their less-than-inspiring prayers.

But what about Jesus? He once prayed, "My God, my God, why have you forsaken me?" (Mark 15:34). If we don't like the way Jesus prayed, we have a much bigger problem. Jesus is supposed to be closer to God than anyone. How could Jesus possibly believe that God had abandoned him? It is bad enough for ordinary human beings to accuse God of forsaking us, to raise hard questions about why God allows terrible things to happen in this world, but what does it mean when Jesus talks like this?

This prayer of Jesus reveals several things:

Jesus was a human being, after all. Whatever we want to say about Jesus' divinity, he was certainly a man who faced a terrible and painful death. It was not just make-believe. He was not an omniscient, omnipotent mind wrapped up in a human body. He was human. And so, when we, too, cry a prayer of despair in our time of trouble, Jesus, who has been there, will be receptive to our plea.

Jesus was praying a prayer from his prayer book, one that he had learned as part of his religious tradition. Psalm 22, of which he quotes the first line, is a lament. And laments are the most common form of prayer in the whole book of Psalms. Though we may, for one reason or another, think that it is unacceptable to come before God in a lament, we should not project our problems with this kind of prayer on Jesus and others who grew up with the Old Testament traditions. It would have been a natural response for a Jew in the situation that Jesus was in to pray a lament.

We should also keep in mind the structure of Psalm 22. Though Jesus is quoted by Mark and Matthew as saying only the first verse of that psalm, we should note that, as with most laments, after a period of complaining and asking for help, the prayer moves on to more positive words of hope and assurance of a hearing and eventual deliverance. And so, the lament is a statement of faith and hope, not only a word of despair.

To say this is not to diminish the reality of Jesus' anguish, but to put it in a context in which it is legitimate to express doubt and anger because of a relationship that is strong enough and broad enough to allow the freedom to struggle.

3.   *Laments have value for us.*

We should tell God what we really think, in spite of all the pressures put on us (often by well-meaning Christian friends) to show only our optimistic side and to suppress any expression of what might be considered negativism—complaining, doubting, anger, or despair. Laments such as those offered by Job, Jesus, David, and Jeremiah affirm the legitimacy of such a prayer. They are valuable to us for a number of reasons.

Laments give us the permission to be honest. As we said earlier, prayer that is not honest is doomed to failure. Many have been relieved to find laments in the Bible. They had felt the pressure to suppress their thoughts. They had worried if they should admit to God what was on their hearts. But if those biblical people, and even Jesus, could talk so openly with God, then it must be all right to take the risk and "tell it like it is."

Recognition of the laments in the Bible puts us solidly in community with other believers—both those who lived long ago and those in the present. People often feel inadequate when they look at others whose faith seems so strong, whose courage never falters, who are never angry, who calmly accept even tragic events in their life. "I guess I'm just not a good Christian," they think. "My faith must be very weak."

Suffering and our reactions to it can be very isolating. We may feel that we are the only ones in the world who have had such terrible thoughts about God. Everyone else seems to handle tragedy better than we do. Then we discover the laments and realize that the great figures of the Bible—even Jesus—had their moments of despair. "So, maybe I'm not so peculiar after all," we say. "Maybe there is even hope for me."

The presence of laments in our Bible is an indication of God's grace. God does not demand perfection before we can approach him in prayer. We are invited to come no matter what our state of mind, though our theologies are confused, though we are in such an emotional turmoil that we spout hostility and spit out curses on real and imagined enemies. We are, in fact, sinners. God knows that, and God is not put off by that. In fact, since we believe that the Bible is God's Word, given to us, even these lament psalms are God's gift to us. God comes to us as we are, desiring honest conversation with us, even providing the words for us to use if we are having trouble forming words of our own.

In some ways, a lament becomes a confession of sin. As long as we refuse to admit that we are this angry, this doubtful, this forlorn, or this self-righteous, repentance and growth are difficult. But if we tell God what we really think, then, sooner or later, we will be able to admit that we are sinners. And if we get our thoughts and feelings out in the open, we can deal with them constructively.

The lament psalms remind us of a process that many must go through in difficult times. Though we do not all react to suffering in exactly the same way, there are certain general stages that describe many persons' pilgrimages through the desert. Often one must have some time to complain, to grieve, to protest, and to descend into the depths and struggle. Only after a period of time which can be shorter or longer, depending on the person, will one be able to hear an encouraging word without dismissing it as a mindless platitude, a naively optimistic piece of fluff.

God does come to people in their distress—as to Job and the psalmist. People do survive, and their faith endures. But the timing is crucial, and we ought not to stifle another's cry of lament until it has had time to run its course.

A lament keeps the door open in our relationship with God. Many have thought that a prayer that begins, "My God, why have you forsaken me?" indicates a lack of trust in God. On the contrary, we could argue that such a prayer is a profound statement of trust, because a person has dared to speak the truth about his or her feelings. It is with those we trust the most that we are willing to let our defenses down and reveal our unpleasant side.

Furthermore, it is an act of great faith to continue praying to God even in times of doubt and anger. In our day many people who are angry with God because of what has happened to themselves or to a loved one turn away from God. Either they doubt God's existence or they refuse to speak to a God who would do such terrible things to people. But it is better to express anger to God than to give up on God. It is very difficult to heal a broken relationship in which conversation has ceased. As long as we keep talking, God will find some way to answer, to break through our brokenness and rage, to tell us once again that we are persons whom God loves and that our future is safe in his hands.

CHAPTER FIVE

ISAIAH 7:10-14
MATTHEW 7:7-11

Dare I Ask for That?

Partly in reaction to the way we hear others pray, some of us have found it hard to know what is a legitimate petition to present to God. We hear others asking for things from God that we would be reluctant to request. Our hesitation comes from two opposite extremes: some requests seem too difficult to be possible; others seem too trivial to take up God's time.

1. *Should we ask for the "impossible"?*

A seminary senior shared her dilemma with the class. On internship she regularly visited an elderly man who was slowly dying of cancer. There was no question that it was terminal. The doctors had done all that they could do. Now it was merely a matter of keeping him as comfortable as possible until the end came. Yet during each visit, he asked her to pray that God would make him well, take away the cancer, and restore his body so that he could lead a normal life again.

She did not know what she should do. She wanted to help him pray his own prayer, but she had a sense of integrity, honesty, and realism that made it difficult to ask for something she knew could not happen. She worried that she would be misleading him, encouraging him to block out the truth about his condition, feeding into his denial system. She thought it would be better if he could face his impending death openly rather than pretend that renewed health was attainable. Furthermore, she was afraid that he was "putting God to the test," pinning his faith in God on a manifestation of God's healing power. If he did not recover, which seemed absolutely certain, would the disappointment and hurt of his unanswered prayer weaken his trust in God and make his imminent death even more terrifying and lonely?

King Ahaz also respectfully refused to put the Lord to the test, even though God had told Ahaz to ask for any sign he wanted, "whether in the deepest depths or in the highest heights" (Isa. 7:11). "You name it," God said, "and I'll do it." Though Ahaz passed up God's offer to ask for the impossible, God decided to give him a sign anyway (Isa. 7:14).

We cannot read the mind of Ahaz to know why he hesitated. Perhaps, to give him the benefit of the doubt, he really did believe it was impertinent for a human being to set up some impossible demand that God must fulfill in order to demonstrate God's power. Or maybe Ahaz did not want to hear the message of the prophet Isaiah and was afraid that if God really did perform a miraculous sign for him, he would have a hard time denying that Isaiah had been sent by God. Or perhaps Ahaz simply did not believe that God could do it. He did not take God at God's word, but rather defined for God what was possible and what was not.

The story of Jesus' temptation by the devil in Luke 4 contains some interesting verbal sparring in which both the devil and Jesus quote Scripture. The devil told Jesus to throw himself down from the top of the temple. "Didn't God promise, through the psalmist [Ps. 91:11-12], that God's angels will guard you, bear you up, and keep your foot from striking against a stone?" the devil asked. He implied that Jesus probably did not trust God completely, or perhaps was not the Son of God after all, if he refused to take God at his word and fling himself from the lofty pinnacle.

Jesus responded in words not much different from Ahaz, quoting Deut. 6:16: "Do not test the Lord your God." Imagine standing atop the tallest building in the city. If you believe in God, God can save you. Throw yourself over the edge and see how strong your faith is—or how foolish you have been. As you pass the 20th floor going down, you may decide that you made a mistake. You have required of God a miracle as a demonstration of God's power. But who are we to test God?

It makes a difference, however, if God offers the sign—as in the case of Ahaz and Isaiah. It is dangerous for us humans to call the shots, to decide what God must do to prove something to us. Worse yet would be to let the devil set the agenda for God's activity in the world.

Should we pray for the "impossible"? Surely. Who are we to say what is impossible? No matter what the odds against our wishes being granted, we are still invited to ask. If the elderly man wants to pray for returned health, then that is what he should pray for.

But as we pray with him, we should listen carefully. Perhaps, after a time, he may change his prayer. The reality of his situation may catch up with him. He may begin to pray less for recovery of health in this life and more for hope in the next life, the serenity to pass easily and painlessly into death, and God's care for loved ones who are left behind. Prayer should be honest communication. Therefore, we should pray for what we really want, not only for what we think is possible. Why should we put limits on God?

We must not, however, put God to the test, saying, "I will believe in you, God, if you pull this off, but if you can't do it, I may lose my faith in you."

The delicate balance is hard to find—on the one hand, ask for the impossible; on the other hand, let God decide what will be done.

2.   Does God want to be bothered with such trivia?

I know a woman who claims that whenever she goes downtown she prays that there will be a parking place within two blocks of her destination. So far, her prayer has always been answered (at least so she claims). More than once I have heard from persons newly moved into my city that God had helped them find an apartment. Many a child has prayed for a new bike or a doll that does whatever the latest dolls are supposed to do. Teenagers have prayed for victory for their football team, a friendly glance from the pretty cheerleader, or a miracle cure for acne.

Are some matters simply too mundane, too unimportant, too common to introduce into our prayers? Doesn't God have better things to do than find parking places for middle-class Americans, driving cars that are too big, looking for fashionable clothes to cram into a closet already filled to capacity? Does God really direct people to apartment houses and nudge mothers to supply every item on the Christmas list? Are there not some items that we should take care of ourselves, quit bothering God about them, and bring only the bigger items to God's attention (like deliverance from death or relief of famine or world peace)? It's hard enough for people nowadays to think about God performing miracles and intervening in affairs of the world without expecting God's participation in petty concerns.

But what is petty and what is important? Who has the right to decide that for us? When Jesus invites us to ask and seek and knock (Matt. 7:7), he does not qualify his invitation by saying we can ask only for things that rank eight or higher on a scale of "what is really significant." If it is important enough for you to want it, pray about it. What is a trivial pursuit for one may be of extreme importance to someone else. A boy may be completely consumed with a passion for that beautiful red bike with the chrome wheel and the 10 speeds. Why shouldn't he, then, be allowed to pray about what is so important to him? To declare such requests out of bounds is to force him to lock off some significant parts of his life and say that God does not care about them.

We ought not to censor our prayers, deciding either what God cannot do (because it is too hard), or what God is indifferent toward (because it is too trivial), and then shaping our prayer to fit such preconceptions. We should pray about what concerns us, and let God decide what to do with it.

3.   *Our prayers can influence God.*

Jesus said, "Ask, and it will be given to you; seek and you will find; knock and the door will be opened to you" (Matt. 7:7). Your prayers make a difference. God hears and responds. In a parallel passage in Luke 11:5-13, Jesus compared God to a man who has already gone to bed for the night when a friend comes to borrow some bread. At first the man refuses the request, because he is snuggled into bed and everything is locked up and he doesn't want to get up. But the friend is so stubbornly persistent that the man finally gives in, crawls out of bed, and gives him what he wants— apparently so he can get rid of him and go back to sleep. This suggests that we should be unrelenting in making our wishes known to God.

The Bible abounds with examples of God being moved to action by the prayers of humans. When the Hebrew slaves cried for deliverance, God heard, sent Moses, and forced the Egyptians to let them go. When the Assyrians heard Jonah's prophecy of doom, they repented, and God heard their prayer and called off their punishment (Jonah 3). Amos twice called on God to hold back the disaster that the people deserved, and twice God listened to him (Amos 7:1-6). The Syrophoenician woman refused to take no for an answer from Jesus when he said that he came to the Jews and not to people like her—even comparing her to a dog. Her perseverance paid off, and her daughter was healed (Mark 7:24-30 and Matt. 15:21-28).

We are to make our requests—big or little, difficult or easy, significant or trivial—with the confidence that they can actually change things. We can have some influence on God and our future by asking for what we want and need.

4.   *Keep in mind some words of caution.*

As we walk carefully through this complex subject, we need to be cautious about a couple of matters: (*a*) human pretension that we can manipulate God, and (*b*) the problem of "unanswered" prayer. In this chapter, we have largely been speaking to those who have backed off from an aggressive sort of prayer that confidently expresses what we want and does not withhold requests that seem to ask for more than we think God can deliver. But, just in case we have made the case from that side too strong, we must briefly note two important distinctions.

Influence and manipulation are not the same thing. Human beings can influence God. God does not respond favorably to our prayer because of some inherent magic in the prayer, as if God, like the genie in the lamp, must do our bidding if we say the right words. God responds because God is moved by our prayer, grieved by our pain, angered by the way others have treated us, gladdened by our confession. God wants only what is best for us. God does not have to do anything that we ask, but God has promised to listen and act on our behalf because of God's love for us.

Prayer is not simply an idle exercise, a completely human process that helps the one who prays feel better, a mere blowing in the wind. There is a God, and God hears the prayer, and God is influenced by the prayer. But, in the end, God is God and will finally do what God wills, no matter what we human beings tell God to do. To think that we can demand and God will jump to our bidding is, indeed, to test God.

It is also important to make a distinction between the legitimacy of our asking and the certainty that we will receive that for which we ask. Underlying all of our questions on this subject is the problem of unanswered prayer. We do not ask for the impossible because we know of too many cases in which people have bucked the odds and prayed for recovery in spite of the doctor's dreadful prognosis, only to have the gloomy prophecy of the medical world prevail over the prayers of the faithful.

The question here is, "Is it all right to ask God for the impossible (or for the trivial)?" And the answer is yes. Do not limit God by prematurely deciding what God can do or what areas of your life are of concern to God.

But that does not mean that you will receive exactly what you requested. We ought not to confuse the open invitation to ask for whatever we want from the Lord with a false assurance that every petition we bring will be granted. To promise the latter is to raise false hopes and to fail to deal with the reality of people's experience.

We will return to look more deeply into this question of unanswered prayer, one of the major issues that affects our prayer life. At this point, we can remind ourselves that prayer is primarily communication with God. Whether or not we receive what we want, whether or not we understand why our request was denied, it is still important that we ask, that we share our inmost thoughts and feelings with God. Furthermore, as we will discuss more fully in a later chapter, even if the answer to our prayer seems to be no, we may find other benefits that have come to us or others, demonstrating that God indeed has heard and answered our prayer.

CHAPTER SIX

AMOS 7:1-9
LUKE 23:32-34

What Good Does It Do to Pray for Others?

We have affirmed that it is all right to pray for oneself. Certainly, it is normal to be concerned for one's own well-being, health, prosperity, security, and emotional and spiritual peace. And there is no request that need be held back. If it is what we want, then we should ask.

But we are also expected to pray for others. The great biblical characters included intercessions for others in their lives of prayer. If prayer is the sharing of our concerns with God, we would be self-centered if it never occurred to us to pray on behalf of other people. Only a very insensitive person could walk through the suffering and pain of this life without feeling a compulsion to pound on God's door, urging God to help those in great need.

Religious people who are alert to the world's pain often find themselves praying for others. It seems the natural thing to do. But does it do any good? How does intercessory prayer affect God? Who, if anyone, is better off because of this kind of prayer? Let us look a little more closely at some of our questions.

1.   There are some difficulties with intercessory prayer.

Some people give the impression that the more numbers you can muster, the more likely you are to achieve the desired result of your prayer. Perhaps if we can mobilize enough people to pray for the same thing, we will be able to force God's hand and accomplish our goal. Very few people would say such a thing directly, but sometimes one detects an underlying assumption that numbers influence prayer's effectiveness. Could it be true that God will pay more attention if there is a large clamor from a multitude than if there is only a hushed individual whisper? We would hardly want to say that, though there may be other benefits in knowing that many people have been praying on your behalf.

Many persons are reluctant to have their private troubles paraded in front of the whole congregation. If a friend knows about our needs and sees fit to mention our name to God, that is fine—as long as it is done in private. We do not want everyone to know about our operation, hemorrhoids, alcoholism, broken family, inability to find a job, or emotional instability. Better to bear one's burdens alone than to have the whole community gossiping about what they learned from the general prayer the previous Sunday. When the pastor begins the worship service by asking if there are any prayer concerns today, many will refuse to let on that there is any issue serious enough to involve the whole church. "It's none of their business," they think.

Some thoughtful persons are disturbed by what intercessory prayer seems to imply about God. God is supposed to have an ear out for the suffering of the least of his creatures, an eye even on the sparrow. Why then should God need to be told about our troubles? And if God knows even before we tell him, then can't God also do something about our needs before we ask? The Creator of the universe should not require direction from mere mortals in order to do what should be done anyway. And so our ideas about an all-knowing, all-caring, all-powerful God are called into question (at least partially) by an assumption that our prayers can effect results that would not be possible without our prayers.

Some people have felt manipulated by those who conceal their desire to control our lives by saying that they are praying for us. "I am praying that God will lead you to make the right choice," they say. I may have already made my decision, but since the person does not agree with me he or she continues to pray that I will change my mind. Or they say, "I am praying that God will give you a wonderful spiritual experience so that you can see the light and leave that wishy-washy church and join up with some true believers."

It is not always good news to know that someone is praying for you. Rather than an expression of concern for our welfare, it may be a none too subtle attempt to control our thinking or behavior—expecially when they take pains to tell us what they have been asking for in their prayers. With considerable skill, they have managed to get God on their side.

There are some troubling issues connected with the idea of praying for other people. We will return to address these matters again when we speak of the benefits of intercessory prayer.

2.   *The Bible gives us examples of intercessory prayer.*

There are many biblical models of people of God praying for the well-being of others. Some of the more noteworthy examples are Abraham, Moses, Samuel, Solomon, Amos, Jeremiah, Job, Jesus, and Paul. Let us highlight episodes in the lives of Abraham, Amos, and Jesus.

Abraham prayed for Sodom (Gen. 18:22-33). Sodom and Gomorrah were notoriously evil cities. God was about to bring destruction upon them as punishment for their terrible deeds. But even in a decadent society like Sodom, Abraham thought, there must be some good people. Abraham took their side and argued with God about the injustice of destroying a whole city if there are some good people there. Abraham appealed to God as the righteous judge of all the earth, who would surely not want to do anything un-fair.

What if there were 50 righteous people there? Would that not be enough to justify saving the city? God agreed.

Abraham went on. What if only 45? Would God destroy the whole city because a mere five good people were missing? God went along with Abraham.

The discussion continued until finally God agreed to spare the city if only 10 people could be found.

Then the conversation abruptly ended. God and Abraham went their separate ways, and the city was destroyed. Why did Abraham stop at 10? Could not even 10 be found? Did God finally put a stop to Abraham's bargaining? Could Abraham move God just so far and no further? Were Lot and his family the only ones who did not deserve to die?

Amos prayed for the kingdom of Israel (Amos 7:1-9). Amos has the reputation of being the hard-nosed prophet of doom, who pronounced terrible words of judgment. But in this passage, we see Amos as an intercessor, the one who pleads with God not to carry out the horrible acts of destruction that the people no doubt deserved.

Amos saw a series of visions—a plague of locusts, a devouring fire, a plumb line for measuring the fitness of a wall. After the first two visions, Amos cried out to God to forgive and to stop the disaster. And, in both cases, God relented and held back the judgment. After the third vision, there is no recorded word of inter-cession from Amos.

As in the episode with Abraham, either Amos did not push it any further, or God was no longer willing to listen. As with Sodom, destruction did come, in spite of the passionate prayers of the intercessor.

Jesus prayed for his enemies (Luke 23:32-34). Hanging there on the cross, slowly dying, experiencing unbelievable pain, Jesus thought of others. Later he would ask some things for himself ("I thirst") and would feel free to express the abandonment that he felt ("Why have you forsaken me?"). But his first concern was to pray for those who had done this to him. "Father, forgive them; for they do not know what they are doing." When most of us would be thinking only of ourselves and our pain, our fear and loss, our hatred toward our enemies, Jesus prayed on their behalf—a profound example of intercessory prayer at its finest. Jesus wanted God to forgive, not react with righteous judgment, not send to hell, even those who had killed God's own Son.

Did God do as Jesus asked? The text does not really say. In the case of Abraham and Amos, there was a temporary reprieve. God wanted to save rather than punish. But in the end even the intercessions of Abraham and Amos could not save Sodom and Israel. Were the pleas of Jesus enough to convince God the Father to forgive the religious leaders, the Roman officials, the vacillating mobs, the betrayer among the Twelve? We don't know.

In all three of these examples, a person who is close to God, who has a gift of communication with God that exceeds that of most of us, instinctively thought of others and prayed on their behalf. Surely, Abraham, Amos, and Jesus did not consider it was an obligation that they should pray for others. Rather, it was the natural thing to do, given their love for human beings and their confidence in God's justice and mercy.

Since most of us are aware that our prayer lives are not as good as could be, we are grateful that holy people, who seem to be in better contact with God than we, also carry our petitions to the Lord. "Pray for me, Pastor," a person may say, assuming (rightly or wrongly) that one who regularly speaks for God from the pulpit should also be able to carry a message in the other direction.

Furthermore, at least in the first two examples, it is clear that God heard the prayer and responded favorably. We can affirm that God is influenced by our prayers, but we cannot say that we are able to manipulate or "sweet talk" God into doing exactly what we want. Though God agreed to deliver Sodom if 10 decent residents could be found, the city finally had to be destroyed. Without repentance on the part of the guilty parties, forgiveness was impossible. The same was true of the Israelites who failed to heed Amos' warning. Surely God could forgive even Judas. But one would suppose that even such a gracious act as that would occur only if Judas repented and desired forgiveness.

We can influence God by our prayers, but we cannot control him. It appears that even God, who wants to work what is best in people's life, is hindered by the stubborn, willful disobedience of human beings.

3.   *Intercessory prayer brings benefits.*

The benefits of intercessory prayer are not restricted to the ones for whom we pray. Though we ought not pray for others in order to gain something for ourselves, there are benefits in praying for others.

Benefits for those who do the praying. Intercessory prayer helps us to look beyond ourselves. Preoccupation with self is a common human problem, especially in times of stress, pain, suffering, or anxiety. But one's own troubles often seem less monumental when seen in the larger picture of what is happening in the lives of other human beings. When we consciously pray for others, our world view broadens. We become more sensitive, more aware of the hurts and needs of the world, not only close at hand among family and friends but in distant and unfamiliar places.

Prayer motivates us to do something to help accomplish that for which we pray. To be sure, there are matters beyond our control that we can only turn over to God. But it would be insincere, if not faithless, to ask something from God that we ourselves are not willing to work to achieve. We pray for world peace, relief from hunger, justice for the oppressed, a nation of which we can be proud, comfort for the grieving and the lonely. Our own prayers should motivate us to action. We should seek ways to bring about what we have asked from God. God may answer our prayers by forcing us to listen to our requests. After all, God does use human beings to achieve God's purposes.

It is good for us to pray for others. It helps us to look beyond ourselves, to gain a larger outlook, to become doers and not just speakers.

Benefits for those on whose behalf we pray. Though God has promised to hear our prayers, the prayer requests may not be granted. Though a million people pray for the same thing, it may not come to pass. As we have said before, there is no guarantee that healing will take place, death will be averted, or peace will break out. But many people have attested that they were greatly comforted by the prayers of others, even if there was no miraculous change in their situation. What was important was to be remembered. And this is where larger numbers can be more effective than fewer numbers. "All those people remembered me," the hurting person can say. "I am not alone. They know and understand what I am going through. They are trying to do something about it."

In times of great trouble, our faith in God is often put to the test. We wonder what kind of God lets his own people endure such misery. God's power and love and concern are called into question. At such times, the prayers of other believers can help us hang on to our belief in a good God. If other human beings are with us, sharing with us, willing to bear our pain and plead for our well-being, then perhaps there is also a God who will take our side, endure our pain, and stand by us to the end. People who pray for us are a living reminder of God's love.

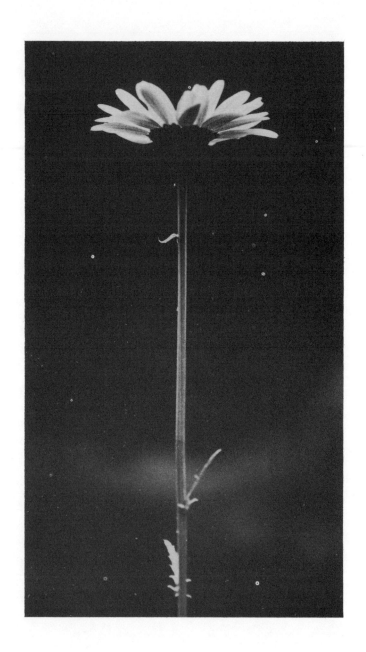

CHAPTER SEVEN

DEUTERONOMY 3:23-28
2 CORINTHIANS 12:7-10

Does God Always Answer Prayer?

The shiny wooden plaque with the folded hands and the gold Gothic script hung over the kitchen sink. The little girl believed the message that was written there: "God always answers prayer." Then one day her dog ran across the street to meet her and didn't see the pickup truck as it came around the corner. She prayed all night for her pet, but he died.

Then, a couple of years later, the doctor said that her grandmother was terribly sick, so they prayed hard for grandma. But a week later she was dead.

Those words on the wall never looked the same to the little girl. She wondered, does God answer prayer or not? She could remember lots of times when her prayers had been answered, but at the two most important times in her life, God had let her down—or maybe it was her own fault for not saying it right, or lacking faith, or being a bad person.

"God always answers prayer." In some ways, that has almost become a platitude. Depending on what you mean when you say it, it is either true or false. Certainly, we do not always receive exactly what we ask for, but it is also true that, in spite of an apparent no from God, many have attested that they have indeed received an answer that was of benefit to them. God answered, all right, but not in the way they had originally hoped.

This directs us to several truths about prayer.

1. Prayer is not merely a list of requests.

One of the reasons that "unanswered" prayer is such a problem for us is because we continue to think of prayer as a laundry list or letter to Santa Claus in which we itemize all those things we want God to do for us or others. We need again to remind ourselves that prayer is communication between two persons in which it is appropriate to talk about all sorts of things that are important to us. It is an opportunity to share our thoughts and feelings, to tell about our good experiences and our failures, to be honest about ourselves, to laugh and to cry. Prayer is not just a list of requests or demands. It would be an odd relationship with a close friend if we talked to her only when we wanted something from her.

Prayer should be part of our lives at all times, not just in periods of crisis when we have exhausted all other possibilities and have no place else to turn but to God. If our relationship with God is deep and continuous, we may still be puzzled and hurt by requests that go unfulfilled, but our relationship with God will probably survive because it will not be dependent on visible evidence of God proving himself by jumping to carry out our instructions.

2.   "Unanswered" prayer need not imply a negative judgment on myself or God.

Even those who insist that "God always answers prayer" must admit that there are exceptions to the rule. However, in order to make some logical sense out of "unanswered" prayer, we often feel compelled to blame someone. It must be someone's fault, or else the prayer would have been granted. But is it my fault, or God's?

One possible explanation for God's refusal to grant my prayer may be that God is angry with me about something. Many people look inward to blame themselves when the promise that God will answer prayer seems not to be kept. "God would not break promises, therefore, I must have done something for which I am being punished," they think. Or, in a slightly different version, "Perhaps God is trying to teach me something. Maybe I need to be humbled, get my priorities straight, quit being so self-centered."

People who are particularly sensitive about guilt, who tend to blame themselves when things go wrong, are especially vulnerable to this way of thinking. "Unanswered" prayer becomes a double burden for them: not only must they continue with the problem that

has not been removed, but they are also convinced
that God would have helped them if they had been
better persons.

Perhaps the problem is my lack of faith. Jesus often
spoke about the power of faith. "Your faith has made
you whole," he said. "If you have enough faith, you
can even remove mountains." Faith healers on tele-
vision insist that if we believe strongly enough, anything is possible. They parade before us fantastic examples of miracles that occurred because people
believed strongly enough. It is as if the power of God
to answer prayer is dependent on our ability to believe
what is possible.

"Unanswered" prayer, then, is caused by our lack
of faith. According to this view, in the way of God's
wonderful and miraculous deeds is our stubborn refusal to believe.

Many people have been terribly hurt by such ideas.
Good pious folk who have been faithful servants of God
all their lives are confronted by a terminal illness. The
doctor tells them the odds. Some of their well-meaning
friends convince them to turn to a noted faith healer
who will surely confound the medical evidence. After
a time it becomes clear that the doctor's prognosis was
correct. Then the dying person is confused, no longer
secure in his relationship with God, wondering why
he could not believe strongly enough when it really
mattered. The well-meaning friends, not willing to
doubt the faith healer and their simplistic view that
sufficient faith can do anything, begin to question their

friend's sincerity. And so, when a person most needs the comfort of God and other human beings, the relationship with both God and friends is shaken by placing the blame for unanswered prayer on the victim.

Maybe God is not as caring as we have been led to believe. Maybe God is really indifferent to our sorrow and suffering. If God really cared, wouldn't God do something to bring relief? Or maybe God is far removed from our daily life. Perhaps God set the world in motion at the beginning, wound it up as a gigantic toy, and then went off into some other corner of the universe, now preoccupied with other projects and too busy to keep an eye on suffering creatures.

These are, of course, perversions of what we teach about a good God who is loving, caring, knowing, and involved in the lives of even the least of us creatures. But, under the stress of "unanswered" prayer, in searching for ways to make sense out of it all, our minds sometimes are pushed toward such unhelpful images of God.

We may misunderstand God's will. Are all things that happen God's will? When I pray for recovery, but the disease becomes chronic and finally terminal, is that God's will? When I pray for peace, but hostility and warfare become even worse, is that God's will? Is it God's will when the parents finally give up on the marriage and seek divorce, in spite of the children's prayers that their mother and father will love each other again?

We sometimes put the phrase "if it be your will" into our prayers. Some people tell us that even to say such a thing indicates a lack of faith on our part, a hedging of our bets, an underlying distrust, a willingness to settle for too little, and, therefore, our prayer is doomed to failure. Others say that such a phrase indicates a trust in God that transcends the way this particular request will be handled and leaves the larger picture up to God, affirming that God has our welfare in mind, no matter what happens.

In the long term, we believe that God's will is done. That is a statement of faith. We hope that God will one day remove all suffering and evil, and we believe that God has the power to bring that about. We know that our future is safe because of that.

But in the short term, in the here and now, we cannot say that every event is willed by God. It cannot be God's will that human beings kill each other in mindless wars, that love between family members turns to hate, that cancer devours once-healthy bodies, that little children are abused by their own parents. Such terrible things happen in this world even when people pray that they will not happen. But that is not to say these things are God's will. If our prayers are not answered, it may not be because God has willed other than what we have requested. God may want the same things we do, but someone or something is working against God's will.

The Bible teaches that sin came into the world through human beings. It was not God's will that the humans turn away from God in defiance, distrust, disobedience. We cannot excuse the terrible things that we do to each other by claiming that they are God's will when they are actually the result of human behavior contrary to God's will. Furthermore, the Bible also recognizes the presence in the world of satanic forces that counteract God's will.

What looks like a no from God may not be an indication that God likes or wills what is happening to us. There may be other explanations why our burden is not removed. In the present time things are taking place that are not God's will. In the long term, however, we remain steadfast in the hope that God's will will be accomplished in its entirety.

3. God said no even to some very saintly people.

Pastors, TV religious personalities, and publications of popular piety constantly remind us of those biblical characters who received positive answers to their prayers. Often those stories make us feel worse as we wonder what is wrong with us because our prayers seem so much less productive.

It may be helpful for us to remember that some very important biblical characters at times did not receive what they asked for. David prayed that his baby son would live, but the infant died anyway (2 Sam. 12:15-23). Jesus prayed in Gethsemane that the cup of suffering be removed from him (Matt. 26:36-46), but there was no way to avoid the cross. Let us look in a little more detail at the experience of two other figures—Moses and Paul.

Moses had led the people of Israel out of Egypt and in the wilderness for 40 years. Before he died, Moses hoped that he would be able to enter the promised land, and he urgently begged the Lord to let that happen. But God said no. Moses could not understand completely why his wish was denied, though he thought that at least one contributing factor was God's anger with the people. God told Moses not to ask anymore for this; it would be beyond his grasp. But what God had to offer to Moses would be sufficient: Moses would be able to get a good look at the land from the top of Pisgah, and God would faithfully carry out his promises to give the people the land through the leadership of Joshua (Deut. 3:23-28).

Even a person of the stature and faith of Moses may not receive what is requested in prayer. Though we may think our prayer is denied, God will provide what is sufficient for our needs. At first it may seem like a poor second choice only to see the land rather than walk on it, but it is something. God says it is enough, and maybe someday we, too, will be satisfied and agree that it is enough. God has indeed answered our prayer, but not in the way we had expected.

Paul was bothered by what he called a thorn in the flesh. We can only speculate what the problem was. Paul said that he pleaded with God three times to have it removed. Three times God said no. Paul, the great missionary of the early church, the one whose writings have shaped the theology of the Christian church for all these centuries, a worthy and faithful servant of the church if there ever was one, could not pray hard enough to compel God to do what Paul wanted. But Paul finally came to the insight that God's grace was sufficient for him. What had seemed a liability, a burden to bear, became an asset. Paul was humbled, forced back on God, inhibited from any temptation to claim great accomplishments for himself. His human weakness made it clear that the spreading of the gospel was God's work. God could use less than perfect human beings, even those with a "thorn in the flesh," in order to work his power in the world (2 Cor. 12:7-10).

Again we are reminded to be honest and realistic in our praying. If even a saint like Paul had to cope with "unanswered" prayer, who do we think we are that we will never have our requests turned down?

Furthermore, as with Moses, it is not so much that the prayer is "unanswered" but that the answer is different from what we expected. Though disappointed not to be relieved of his "thorn," Paul finally came to see that even this unpleasantness could be an asset because God used it to teach him something. God had answered him after all.

4. Live with the mystery.

We do not always know why our prayers remain unanswered. Perhaps it is best not to push so hard for an explanation that we lock ourselves into a cycle of blame, assuming some deficiency in ourselves, or that God lacks concern, knowledge, or power. We do better to accept that the reason our prayers are denied is a mystery—especially when what we want should be the same as God wants (like the removal of suffering, the comforting of a troubled spirit, or the curtailing of evil humans). It is all right to leave these questions open, to admit and express our disappointments and fears and doubts. A lament is still an appropriate prayer to bring to God in times of struggle.

Does God always answer prayer? No and yes. Obviously, our specific petitions may not be granted, but we will receive something—an answer, if you will. And it will be sufficient. We will know that God is present, that God has heard, that we are not alone. We will be given strength to cope. We may even be further blessed with new insights and renewed faith. Though we still may continue to wish for more, we will learn to be grateful for what God has given, and we will know that in a profound way our prayer has been answered.

CHAPTER EIGHT

PSALM 6:4-5
LUKE 17:1-10

Does God Need Our Thanks and Praise?

Every year the routine was the same. On his birthday his mother's aunt Julia sent him clothes, and at Christmas she sent a book. He was never surprised, but he always marveled at how unfashionable were the clothes and how boring was the book. She never bothered to check what boys his age were wearing, and she didn't know him well enough to understand how inappropriate was her choice of reading material.

Worst of all, he had to write the traditional thank-you letter. His mother was a stickler about that. "Aunt Julia will be hurt if you don't tell her how much you liked her present," she would say. "She always remembers you. It's the thought that counts." He was forced to thank his aunt for something he didn't really want in order to make her feel better.

Authors who write books about how to get other people to do what you want them to do tell us that we should praise their successes. In most cases the carrot works better than the stick. The worker will be more productive, the student better motivated, the child more likely to clean her room, if we articulate our pleasure over their accomplishments.

Although this is a true and helpful insight, such advice often borders on manipulation, using people, playing on their need for affirmation and praise in order to achieve what we want from them.

Because we tend to draw analogies from our human relationships in order to understand our relationship with God, we may wonder if God is like Aunt Julia (who needs to be thanked or she will feel neglected) or the salaried worker in the office (who needs to be praised for past achievements before we can get anymore out of him). Does God need our worship, our thanksgiving and praise? Is God like an oriental king who expects people to grovel at his feet and recite over and over what a wonderful and generous benefactor he is? Does God have that kind of ego? Or, do we praise God in order to set God up for future requests?

1. God does not need our praise, but probably likes it.

We try to make God in our own image. We imagine that God has needs like ours. One way to understand sacrifice in the ancient world was to think of it as a way of satisfying God's hunger or thirst. If we feed

God, then God will do something for us. In Psalm 50
God set the people straight on this matter. "I don't
need any animals from your flocks," God said (v. 9).
"Every living creature belongs to me. It is ridiculous
that I should depend on human beings to provide me
with food (vv. 10-11). Even if I was hungry, I wouldn't
tell you" (v. 12). Similarly, God spoke through Amos
to tell the people that he hated their worship services,
and he would not listen to their liturgies nor accept
their offerings (Amos 5:21-23). You cannot buy God.
You cannot flatter with praise or sway with your mi-
serly offerings the one who not only made and owns
the gifts you bring but even made you, the giver. What
really counts with God is justice and righteousness
(Amos 5:24). If you want to impress God, try living
justly and lovingly with one another.

Some of the lament psalms may also give the impression that God really likes to be praised and would miss
praise if it were absent. When people are in deep
trouble, they sometimes say and do things that in normal times they would never consider. Stress may push
a person into bargaining with God, as in Ps. 6:4-5.
First, the psalmist asked for God's deliverance for the
sake of God's steadfast love (v. 4). That is a very right
and proper thing to do. God has promised to love us
with a consistent, unwavering love, and we should
appeal to those promises when we come to God to ask
for the removal of our trouble.

But then the psalmist went on to say that in death
there is no remembrance of God. In those days most
people did not believe in individual life after death.

When you died you were dead. And, said the psalmist, "Who praises you from the grave?" (v. 5). This assumes that God wants to be praised. If God wants me to join in praise, then God better do something to help very quickly, or I'll be dead, and the choir lifting praises toward God will be reduced by at least one voice.

God does not need our praise. Human beings may be in constant need of affirmation, words of encouragement, praise for tasks well done. We may respond to flattery and be vulnerable to manipulation by those who know how to butter us up. But God is not a human being. Amos and the other prophets were right when they heard God denounce efforts to control God by worship and sacrifice. The lament psalms (like Psalm 6) shows us how pervasive is our desire to influence God through whatever means possible, so that we even attempt to appeal to God's vanity.

But God does seem to want our praise. God has tied himself closely to us creatures and loves us and is affected by what we do with our lives. Surely God is displeased when we turn away and never return thanks to the giver of all life's gifts. God is no doubt pleased when we remember who we are and who God is and speak to God about that. To say that God does not need our praise is not to say that God does not want it, though more for us than for God.

In Luke 15, we read several parables about the delight God finds in the return of the one who had been lost—the sheep, the coin, the prodigal son. God rejoices when one who has not been offering praise suddenly comes to his senses and renews a right relationship with God. The ensuing praise delights God, not for God's sake, but for the sake of the one who had lost the sense of praise but now has found it again.

2. A thankful and joyful attitude is for our own good.

It is not God who benefits from the praises we offer; we are the ones who gain. When we take time to put into words the blessings in our life, we grow in appreciation of all that has been given to us. If we never bother to name those things for which we are thankful, we are probably taking them for granted, and our life is more confining, less open to the joys of living, than it could be. In our prayers we should consciously articulate the reasons for offering God praise—for our own good, not just because God wants or expects it.

A stance of praise and thanksgiving reminds us of our dependence on God. Good things that happen to us are not necessarily something we have earned, deserved, or have a right to expect. They are gifts from God. A person who is always open with praise toward God is one who recognizes our human dependence on our Creator and Redeemer.

God gives the gifts anyway, whether or not we give thanks. God will not take back the blessing if we do not show proper gratitude. In Luke 17:11-19 we read about ten lepers who were cleansed by Jesus. Only one, a Samaritan, returned to give thanks. There are many interesting layers of meaning in this story. The fact that the only one who expressed his thanks was a Samaritan is significant; an outsider was more appreciative of Jesus' miracle than those who were already within the religious community.

God's gift of healing was not contingent on the thanks offered by the recipients. Apparently all ten were still rid of their leprosy. So, what advantage does the one have over the other nine who did not return? The story does not provide further details. But one could assume that the thankful eyes through which the Samaritan viewed the world would make his life more exciting and open to God than that of the nine who were still so out of touch with God that they didn't even know enough to recognize the source of their good fortune.

3.   For what do we give God praise?

As we seek to heighten our sense of appreciation for life and our dependence on the good God who has given it, biblical prayers can provide some helpful guidelines. Generally speaking, biblical psalms of praise give glory to God for two main reasons—the gift of creation and God's work on our behalf in history.

Psalm 104 is an example of a hymn to God the Creator. God is praised as the one who made the heavens, the clouds, the wind and rain and lightning. God made the world a secure place to live, putting boundaries around the destructive flood waters but providing springs and rain for the growth of grass and food and trees. Everything works with precision. The heavenly bodies mark the seasons; all animals and humans have their proper place in this wonderfully constructed world.

Many of us walk blindly through life without really observing the wonders all around us and within us—

the bright green of a spring morning, the baby ducks on the pond, the stone-cold ground warmed by the sun until it brings forth food to please our taste and strengthen our bodies, the complicated interworking of heart and lung and liver and kidneys that keeps us alive and well without our even giving it a thought. To sing praise is to name and more fully value what we have been given.

Similarly we praise God for what God has done in the history of the world. Particularly as a religious community we praise God for those extraordinary events in which God was seen most clearly: the escape from oppression in Egypt, and the death and resurrection of God's own Son. But we also have our personal reasons to thank and praise God, our own list of persons and events in which God has become visible to us. We look back and thank God for the wonders wrought in our own lives, and we see, though sometimes only from a considerable distance, how God's hand has been present throughout our journey.

4. How do we praise God when nothing good has happened lately?

I shall never forget the prayer my father offered at our evening meal on the day my mother died. The words that stand out in my memory, as a 14-year-old at the time, were something like: "We thank you, God, for all your wonderful blessings."

"Why is he saying that?" I wondered. "What is so wonderful about losing a mother and wife at an unnaturally early age? What kind of a blessing is this?"

But that example of piety, of faith in the midst of adversity, has stuck with me all these years—sometimes causing discomfort because of my own inability to be grateful when things have gone badly.

What do we do when bad things are happening? Do we praise God, anyway—carrying on as if everything is still all right, mouthing words of praise even when we are angry with God for letting it all turn out this way?

Sometimes the creation seems to have gone off its ordered course. In one area floods destroy, while in other places drought prevails. Tornadoes, hurricanes, and earthquakes bring inexplicable horror, often to poor people who are least able to cope with such disasters. As fast as we develop cures for one illness, new ones take their place.

We look for evidence of God working in the world and wonder what God has done for us lately. So God saved the people of Israel from domination by Egypt, but what about all those people living under totalitarian tyrannies in our own day? Though Jesus healed the bodies and spirits of many in those days, what about our loved ones who die premature and painful deaths or who endure meaningless lives of boredom or anxiety or depression?

Some would have us praise God anyway. There is, no doubt, some value in such advice. We can always find some things for which to be grateful. Looking for reasons to be thankful may help us rise from ruts of doom and gloom so that we again see the beauty that life continues to offer. But we must be careful not to turn this into a commandment, not to force people to lie to God, concealing their true thoughts in a desperate effort to be upbeat when it is impossible.

The lament prayers are appropriate at a time like this—a time when one wants to praise but cannot, a time when one waits for the old assurances of God's providence to return. It has been said that a lament is praise of God in the absence of God. It is a way of keeping the conversation open, turning to the one who can help, keeping alive the glimmer of faith that motivates us to pray at all. The lament is a transition on the way back to a more conventional hymn of praise or thanksgiving.

As Christians, even in our times of deepest trouble, we have special reason to praise God. We know a God who has identified fully with our suffering, who has walked the way of the cross, who has experienced pain and endured the unknown of death, but who has won the victory over all that can hurt us. And so we are able to give praise to God even when everything has gone wrong. This is possible because the story of Jesus on the cross embodies for us in the most profound way the presence of God in our own times of suffering, and because God's victory at Easter makes it absolutely clear that suffering is not the last word and not even death can defeat us. As God won that battle, so, God will do for us. Since we know that, there is never a time in which we cannot give praise and thanks to God.